F*CK IT, I'M BUYING A CABIN

written by **Jesse Regis**   illustrated by **Stephanie Sosa**

100 BLOCK
BY ROW HOUSE

When she was growing up
Sarah believed she could be...

a detective...

a teacher...

Dr. Kelleher Ph.D.

But with class after class
and loan after loan
Sarah's debt piled up,
Forget buying a home!

So Sarah moved to the city
looking for a new life.
But found cat-sized rats
and broken crack pipes.

A sink stacked with dishes,
the floor brown and sticky,
a secret boyfriend always over,
giving Elder Brian a hickey.

A shoebox apartment
with three skeevy roomates,
a chef, a Mormon,
an actor 40 years late.

They bickered and fought,
even came close to blows.
Stuffed in cramped spaces,
roommates soon became foes.

She'd escape on long walks,

but could barely go a mile,

without catcalls and whistling,

And at her tech job,
it grew harder to care.
Lousy pay, endless hours–
Corporate life's a nightmare.

Ping-pong and bad coffee,
with no raise and no bonus.
There was only one choice.
Sarah gave two-weeks' notice.

Hell is other people!
She'd choose to be alone—
move to the mountains
and call that her home.

Sarah found a realtor.
She was ready to commit.
He was kind and compassionate
and *hardly* glanced at her tits.

They drove past cafes,
thrift stores, and candle shops,
two thousand square feet for olive oil–
Holy shit, a mom and pop!

But nothing stood out.
She was all out of luck.

She'd suffer the city.
It didn't *all* suck.

She turned to her journal,
writing everything down,
time with friends, happy memories,
the bar crawls downtown.

How could she leave?
She felt unbearable weight.

Would she drain her life savings
to buy real estate?

Down payments, insurance, mowing lawns, cleaning gutters, property taxes, hippie neighbors who churn their own butter?

The anxiety was building
"This bra is too tight!"
Exhausted and restless—
sleep meds every night.

As she lay there,
thoughts cluttered her head.
But then, suddenly, clarity!
Sarah sprang out of bcd.

The city was fun.
She loved her best friends.
But she must put herself first.
This toxic shit has to end.

And she liked the outdoors, disappearing off-grid.

She hated her cell phone and for sure didn't want kids.

So the city was out,
Townie life was a *no*.

She felt helpless and hopeless.

Where could she go?

She took a deep breath.

I'm making this happen!

Sarah gathered her courage,

F*CK IT,
I'm buying a cabin!

Library of Congress Cataloging-in-Publication Data Available Upon Request

Illustrations and layout design by Stephanie Sosa

ISBN: 9781955905329; eISBN: 9781955905497

Published by 100 Block by Row House, an imprint of Row House Publishing
Distributed by Simon & Schuster
Printed in the United States

Fonts used in the design of this book:
Tomarik and Apolline
The artwork was created using Procreate.

First edition
10 9 8 7 6 5 4 3 2 1

Jesse Regis is the founder of the fun and subversive Virgins On Fire Candle Co. A New Jersey boy, Regis was a fundraiser for one of the best art and design colleges in the country and the largest community-based food pantry in New York City. He was also a community organizer on a winning presidential campaign. Regis earned a degree in political science from George Washington University and lives in Brooklyn, NY, with his partner and their rescue dog son, Rockwell "Rocky" Rufferman.

Stephanie Sosa is a biracial illustrator who uses design to explore cultural identity and social theory. She earned a degree in graphic design from North Carolina State University and is currently based in Raleigh, NC. Outside of her design work, you can find her teaching piano lessons, volunteering with Sino diaspora organizations, and making conversation with just about anyone.